With love to our little angel, Zach
~ Mimi

THE WISE ANIMAL HANDBOOK

Kate B. Jerome

ARCADIA KIDS

Attempt
new
skills
from
time
to
time.

Just **try** to think them **through.**

And if you **find** you're left **behind**...

...then change your point of view.

Try
not
to
think
of just
yourself.

Invent new ways to share.

Stay close to friends whom you can trust.

But
always
be
aware.

Avoid
the
tattle
in the
tale.

Insist that **truth** is **best.**

Embrace with pride the strengths you have.

Demand
to be
impressed.

Enjoy the peace that nature brings.

Ignore what's just for show.

Join **forces** when the road gets **rough.**

Admit
when you
don't know.

Remember **family** is the **best.**

Despite the ups and downs.

Don't **hide** from things
that you must **face.**

Make
joyful
laughing
sounds.

Eat **healthy** food to **grow** up **strong.**

Be **patient** with your **friends.**

Try not to take a stubborn stand.

Be
quick
to make
amends.

Excuse
yourself
when
manners
slip.

Be helpful every day.

Keep trying even when it's hard.

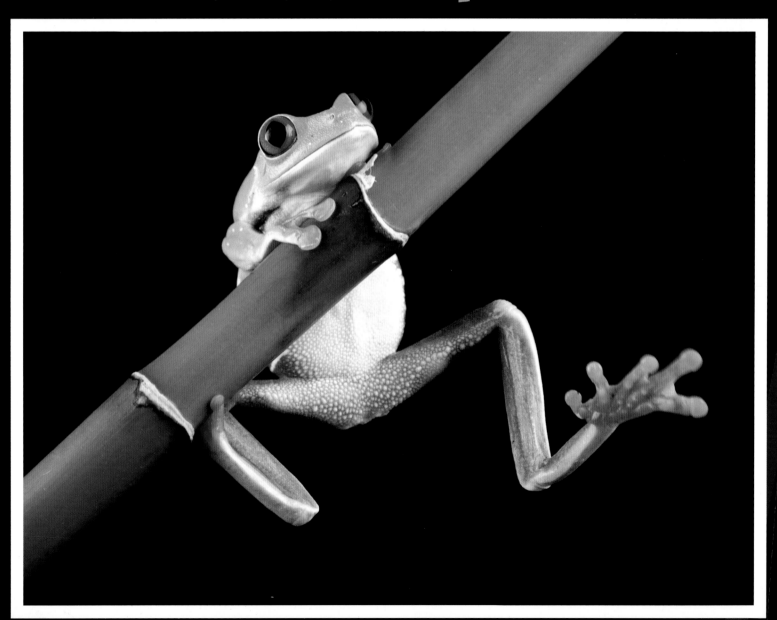

But don't forget to play!

And

sing

...and **dance** each **day!**

Written by Kate B. Jerome
Design and Production: Lumina Datamatics, Inc.
Coloring Illustrations: Tom Pounders
Research: Eric Nyquist

Cover Images: See back cover

Interior Images: 002 Anetapics/Shutterstock.com; 003 George Green/Shutterstock.com; 004 Sergey Uryadnikov/Shutterstock.com; 005 Gnomeandi/Shutterstock.com; 006 Bruce MacQueen/Shutterstock.com; 007 Henk Bentlage/Shutterstock.com; 008 M.M./Shutterstock.com; 009 Mikael Damkier/Shutterstock.com; 010 Brendan van Son/Shutterstock.com; 011 Michael Pettigrew/Shutterstock.com; 012 StevenRussellSmithPhotos/Shutterstock.com; 013 Pakhnyushchy/Shutterstock.com; 014 Patjo/Shutterstock.com; 015 Quinn Martin/Shutterstock.com; 016 Lincoln Rogers/Shutterstock.com; 017 Dirk Ercken/Shutterstock.com; 018 Karel Gallas/Shutterstock.com; 019 Orangecrush/Shutterstock.com; 020 Guenter-foto/Shutterstock.com; 021 Janecat/Shutterstock.com; 022 Shironina/Shutterstock.com; 023 Annette Shaff/Shutterstock.com; 024 Vitaly Titov/Shutterstock.com; 025 Rohappy/Shutterstock.com; 026 MattiaATH/Shutterstock.com; 027 Otsphoto/Shutterstock.com; 028 FikMik/Shutterstock.com; 029 Four Oaks/Shutterstock.com; 030 Ekaterina Kolomeets/Shutterstock.com; 031 Hugh Lansdown/Shutterstock.com.

Published by Arcadia Kids, a division of Arcadia Publishing and
The History Press, Charleston, SC

For all general information contact Arcadia Publishing at:
Telephone: 843-853-2070
Email: sales@arcadiapublishing.com

For Customer Service and Orders:
Toll Free: 1-888-313-2665
Visit us on the Internet at www.arcadiapublishing.com

Library of Congress Cataloging-in-Publication data is on file with the publisher.

Printed in China

A NorCal **Land Mammal**

Tule Elk

Read Together

Point Reyes National Seashore Park in NorCal is the only National Park where tule elk can be found.

A NorCal **Marine Mammal**

California Sea Otter

Read Together

When California sea otters rest, they often wrap themselves in kelp to keep from drifting away.

A Rare NorCal Bird

California Clapper Rail

Read Together

The California Clapper Rail lives mainly in the marshes around San Francisco Bay. These birds are rare and like to hide, so consider it a treat if you see one!

A NorCal Amphibian

Rough-Skinned Newt

Read Together: This little amphibian may look sweet, but it has a poison in its body to keep other animals from eating it. So don't go near this NorCal newt!